Original title:
Bark Banter

Copyright © 2025 Creative Arts Management OÜ
All rights reserved.

Author: Aidan Marlowe
ISBN HARDBACK: 978-1-80567-372-9
ISBN PAPERBACK: 978-1-80567-671-3

Conversations Underneath the Canopy

Squirrel on the branch, what a sight,
Chatting with the breeze, feeling light.
Paws up high, tails they wag,
With secrets shared, no reason to brag.

Leaves rustle softly, jokes take flight,
Laughter echoes in the dappled light.
A witty quip, a playful tease,
Nature's humor floating with the breeze.

Underneath the trees, tales unfold,
Of daring leaps and fetches bold.
While shadows play, we jest and rhyme,
Outsmarted by a butterfly, every time!

From roots to tips, we giggle and cheer,
The woods our stage, with friends so dear.
With every bark and every grin,
The forest's laughter draws us in.

Fetching Memories

Chasing tails and playful wags,
Moments captured in happy lags.
Sticks and balls, our joys prevail,
Fetching laughter on the trail.

Puppy eyes gleam with delight,
Every leap a joyous sight.
Fleeting memories stitched in time,
Laced together with every rhyme.

Whispers of adventures past,
Each fetch a story, shadows cast.
With muddy paws and grass-stained fur,
We share our tales with a joyful purr.

And as the sunset paints the sky,
We gather 'round, no need to shy.
With playful nudges and gentle grins,
Fetching memories, where it all begins.

The Gathering of Growls

Round the tree, a troupe assembles,
With curious barks and playful trembles.
Witty growls and tiny yips,
In our secret spot, laughter flips.

From every corner, friends arrive,
With wagging tails, we come alive.
Sniff and snicker, a chat takes form,
In our cozy nook, a lively swarm.

Jokes shared over fallen leaves,
As autumn whispers, everyone believes.
A spin of tales, a playful tease,
In this gathering of barks, we find our ease.

With gleeful howls into the night,
Underneath the stars, oh, what a sight!
Our growls, a symphony, wild and free,
In the chorus of delight, just you and me.

Brews of Barks and Boughs

Under leafy boughs, we brew our fun,
With a sprinkle of mischief, it's never done.
With cups of cheer and jolly barks,
We sip sweet moments in playful parks.

The sun dips low, the night calls near,
With tales exchanged, we hold them dear.
Laughter spills like an evening gust,
In this pot of joy, we place our trust.

Ears perked up, we listen close,
To every bark that makes us boast.
The warmth of bonds, in stories told,
A blend of hearts, both new and old.

So gather 'round, let the giggles flow,
In this merry mix, let's steal the show.
With each wag and woof, let's raise a cheer,
In the brews of laughter, we hold so dear.

A Chorus of Canine Companions

In the park they prance and play,
Chasing tails and dreams all day.
With wiggly butts and silly barks,
They fill the air with joyful larks.

One spots a squirrel, oh what a chase!
The rest join in with silly grace.
They tumble down, a furry heap,
While humans laugh, and some just weep.

Their noses twitch, with tales to tell,
Of chew toys lost and trees they fell.
Each woof a story, each wag a smile,
Together they roam, mile after mile.

So here's to the canines, all in a row,
With floppy ears and tails that flow.
In their world of fun, they're always fine,
A chorus that makes our hearts align.

Between the Roots and the Sky

Under trees they sniff and snuff,
For secret tales and scents so gruff.
A tug-of-war with a chewed-up shoe,
Who knew the joy in a friendly stew?

They leap like frogs and roll like stew,
The world a stage for a daring crew.
With leaps and bounds, they steal the show,
As butterflies dance, and breezes blow.

A squirrel chatters, they tilt their heads,
With playful barks, they forge their threads.
A comedy act in fur and grace,
In nature's lap, they find their place.

Among the roots that twist and twine,
They plot and scheme, and scheme just fine.
With every paw, they write a tale,
Of friendship strong, that'll never pale.

Friendship in Fur and Fronds

Furry pals with wagging tails,
In the garden where laughter prevails.
Rolling in grass with joy so bright,
Chasing the shadows, they're quite a sight.

A little bark, a mischief's tease,
They dance with flowers in the breeze.
Swapping toys like a trading fair,
Companionship fills the sunlit air.

From muddy puddles to bright blue skies,
Their bonds grow tight, like superhero ties.
Each little woof, a melody sweet,
With every hop, they bring the heat.

So here's to fur in leafy shades,
And whimsy filled with sunlit glades.
In laughter and play, they find their blend,
In fur and fronds, on joy they depend.

The Council of the Canines

In a secret spot beneath the trees,
The canines gather with utmost ease.
With noses low and tails held high,
They plot and plan, oh me, oh my!

With barks and yips, they form a vote,
On who should fetch the biggest coat.
Tails a-wagging, they take their stance,
With goofy grins, they leap and dance.

One hound suggests a game of chase,
While another dreams of conquering space.
Each idea met with silly rants,
As they roll in grass like happy ants.

The council laughs, their hearts so light,
For every bark brings pure delight.
In furry unity, their spirits soar,
In their joyful realm, they ask for more.

Paws and Poetry

In a yard where dogs do play,
An epic tale of woofs today.
With wagging tails and silly snores,
They share their dreams and open doors.

Each pup has quirks, oh what a sight,
As they chase shadows in the light.
With playful barks and joyous leaps,
Their laughter echoes, and the fun keeps.

A squirrel darts, they race with glee,
What's more amusing than this spree?
The finest rhymes, paws on the ground,
In furry jest, pure joy is found.

Echoing Barks at Dusk

As daylight fades, the chase begins,
A chorus of howls, the night's loud wins.
Fleecy friends, with eyes aglow,
In twilight's playground, they'll steal the show.

With yelps and grunts, they weave a tale,
Of phantom tails and moonlit trails.
Each bark a joke, each whimper fun,
They're the stars of the evening run.

In the garden, where shadows play,
A chorus of giggles chases the day.
Each echo rings with spirits bright,
Monkeys, squirrels, all take flight!

The Hidden Harmonies of Hounds

In corners quiet, pups conspire,
With wiggly butts, they never tire.
They plot their pranks, a clever crew,
With sniffs and nudges, what will they do?

A playful growl, a sneaky glance,
Each dog a star in this comic dance.
With sticky paws and floppy ears,
Their giggles drown our grown-up fears.

With hidden treasures in the grass,
They share their wealth in a puppy class.
A stick, a ball, a chewed-up shoe,
In this symphony, they all break through.

Paws Against the Earth

In fields so green, with tails a-wag,
Each pup is ready for a brag.
They dig and jump, roll in the dirt,
With mud-splash splendor, they won't get hurt.

Their goofy grins are hard to miss,
With every leap, there's bliss.
Chasing sunbeams, in joyful races,
Knocked-down flowers, a win for furs and faces.

They bark a song, so rich and wild,
As nature laughs, each puppy styled.
With hearts so light and spirits free,
They mark their joy for all to see.

Playful Paws and Pithy Paws

In the yard, they zoom around,
Tiny feet, a playful sound.
Chasing tails, they flip and dive,
In this world, they come alive.

A woof here, a yip there,
Sniffing for secrets everywhere.
With wiggly butts, they prance,
A circus act, a silly dance.

Each toss of a ball, they cheer,
Furry clowns, they bring us near.
With every leap, they spread delight,
Our fluffy buddies, pure and bright.

Heavy Hounds and Lighthearted Howls

Big and bold, they lumber by,
Heavy paws that touch the sky.
With gentle eyes, they always tease,
A playful nudge, a cheeky breeze.

Their howls echo into the night,
Chasing shadows, what a sight!
A moonlit stage for silly views,
Belly flops, and playful snooze.

They plop down hard, a woofy thud,
Rolling over in the mud.
With wagging tails, they turn and spin,
Laughing softly, let the fun begin!

Moonlit Mischief and Canine Quips

Under the stars, they plot their schemes,
Chasing dreams, like wild beams.
A tap dance here, a gentle paw,
With twinkling eyes, they break the law.

Sneaking snacks and stealing toys,
These cheeky pups, all giggles and noise.
With every wiggle, a story unfolds,
Furry jesters, with hearts of gold.

They tease the shadows with barking glee,
In their world, forever free.
Mischief glimmers in their gaze,
Lighting up our doggy days.

The Rhythm of Paws and Laughter

Pitter patter, paws at play,
A joyous dance, come what may.
With the rhythm of their furry feet,
They create our happy beat.

Each bark a note, each leap a song,
Together they make our hearts feel strong.
In sunny fields, they frolic and chase,
With goofy grins, they set the pace.

Through puddles splash, they race and spin,
With every giggle, oh, where to begin?
These furry friends, what a treasure,
In every moment, purest pleasure.

Canine Chronicles of the Night

Under the stars, they prance around,
Chasing shadows, making silly sounds.
With a wagging tail and a playful sigh,
They plot mischief as the moon climbs high.

Squirrels whisper secrets from the trees,
While dogs plan how to rustle the leaves.
Each barking laugh dances on the breeze,
Their nighttime antics sure to please.

A raccoon peeks out, nose twitching wide,
But with a loud woof, the dogs all glide.
They leap in joy, no critter to hide,
In the moonlit glow, their spirits abide.

With dreams of bones and stars in their eyes,
They race and tumble under night skies.
Each woof a tale, each wag a cheer,
In these chronicles, fun times appear.

Mischievous Paws and Moonlight Chat

Two playful pups plot under the moon,
With sly little grins, they'll be howling soon.
A wag of the tail, a mischievous glance,
They orchestrate their nightly dance.

Socks left outside become their delight,
Snatching and tugging with all of their might.
Woofs and yips fill the midnight air,
In their joyful romp, it's pure canine flair.

Beneath the glow of a flickering lamp,
They trade silly stories with a playful stamp.
Each paw on their journey leaves laughter behind,
In the tales of the night, they're perfectly aligned.

From barks to giggles, the moon holds witness,
To tales spun with joy, they're boundless in fitness.
With a woof and a wag, their friendship is strong,
In the magical night, they truly belong.

Tales from the Canine Campfire

Gather 'round, furry friends of the night,
With tales of mischief that bring pure delight.
Around the campfire, they sit in a line,
Each dog has a story, and all will be fine.

"Once I chased a cat," one puppy will brag,
"It climbed up a tree, like a cheeky little nag!"
The crowd erupts in a chorus of barks,
Each tale shared is a spark that ignites.

With grins on their muzzles, and tails all a-wag,
They boast of their deeds with each happy brag.
From slippery puddles to strange smells unexpected,
Their laughter and barkings feel quite connected.

As the fire crackles, the moon gives a glow,
With paws all around, the fun starts to flow.
From howls to stumbles, they share in delight,
At this canine campfire, all feels just right.

Fables of the Furrowed Brow

In the yard where the sunflowers sway,
A curious pup ponders his play.
With a frown on his face, he surveys the ground,
Wondering where all his lost toys are found.

"Why must the cat be such a tease?"
He scoffs at the thought, "Is it me she sees?"
With sticky paws on a tall garden fence,
His quest for fun seems quite intense.

Every rustle brings forth a sudden chase,
With furrowed brow, he's set at a pace.
He darts and he dives, with a yip or a growl,
Finding laughter in each playful prowl.

At dusk when the sky starts to change hue,
He lays down his head, with fun tales anew.
With dreams filled with bones and friends by his side,
In this mischievous world, he'll always abide.

Frolicsome Fables from the Four-Legged

A dog with a sock, on a quest for the shoe,
In stealthy pursuits, he leaps with a view.
The cat gives a glare, all fluff and all ire,
But the hound just bounds with zest, never tire.

In parks, they embark on adventures so grand,
Chasing their tails as they frolic in sand.
The squirrels just giggle, their antics bemuse,
While the gang rolls about, like a scene that's cartooned.

A puddle of joy, a splash and a howl,
The mischief creates quite the raucous growl.
One leaps for a stick, another snags treats,
All together, a patchwork of wagging heartbeats.

The sun sets in colors that dance on their fur,
Happy little howls and a flurry of whir.
With laughter so loud, as the moon starts to rise,
The tales of these pups light the night with their sighs.

Joyful Journeys of the Pooch Pack

Off they go, the furry brigade,
With noses a-twitching, no plans well laid.
Each corner a treasure, each leaf a delight,
Chasing their dreams in the morning's soft light.

Their barks weave a song, the rhythm of play,
While tails wave like flags, in a grand display.
The golden retriever starts a race on a whim,
But it ends in a tumble—oh dear, look at him!

A game of fetch turns to great comedy,
The stick turns to a log that's stuck in a tree.
With exaggerated leaps and some clumsy spins,
They roll in the grass with broad, goofy grins.

Back home as the sun dips, they nap in a heap,
Dreaming of shenanigans that make their hearts leap.
Their journey concludes with a satisfied sigh,
As playful pup laughs echo under the sky.

Whispers of the Woodland

In the woodland neat, where the critters convene,
Two pups share secrets under leaves so green.
With whispers and wiggles, their tales intertwine,
Of frogs that sing songs, and of trees that shine.

One claims a squirrel stole his very best bone,
But the other just giggles, "That's just how they've grown!"
They craft clever plots to reclaim what's theirs,
Being champions of jest, with laughter that shares.

A bushy-tailed thief makes a daring grand run,
Chasing through brambles, oh what fun, what fun!
Their paws leave a trail of joy in the air,
As nature's own jokers, they dance without care.

In twilight's embrace, they return to their nook,
With whispers of friendship in every hook.
A howl to the moon, in the dusky moonlight,
Their woodland adventures are pure delight.

Canine Conversations

Two pups sit down for a chat in the grass,
The sun shines bright while the minutes just pass.
With paws all a-wagging, they discuss their great day,
How the mailman ran fast, oh, what a ballet!

"One jumped like a jackrabbit, the other a cat,
I swear I could smell a pizza from Matt!"
A giggle ensues, with a snort and a yelp,
As they share all their tales with a joyous yelp.

They ponder the mystery of squirrels that tease,
Debating the merits of chasing with ease.
"Not all of them scurry, some actually stare,"
Said one with a wink and a chuckle to spare.

As the daylight fades, their chatter still hums,
Of dreams that are whiskers and treats that are crumbs.
With chuckles and woofs, they call out to the night,
These canine companions, a marvelous sight.

Nocturnal Natter of the Brave

When the moon is high and bright,
Dogs in the dark share tales of fright.
With shadows dancing on the wall,
They whisper secrets, big and small.

A cat creeps by, with stealth and grace,
They stop and stare, a funny face.
The bravest hound lets out a howl,
While others giggle, eyes a-scowl.

In the bushes, squirrels snicker loud,
As pups prance 'round, feeling proud.
Their nightly gossip makes them bold,
As stories of mischief unfold.

So here's to those who roam at night,
With wagging tails, they find delight.
In every bark and every yip,
A world of laughter, on a trip.

The Silent Stories of Sniffed Streets

On the corner where shadows meet,
A mighty sniff gives tales a seat.
Each tree holds whispers, tales so grand,
Of all the dogs that crossed this land.

With tails a-wagging, they share the news,
Of sneaky cats and other ruse.
Barking softly, they ponder a tale,
While night air carries a muffled wail.

But oh, the antics that dogs unfold,
With eyes wide open, their hearts are bold.
From chasing tails to the latest craze,
Each sniffing secret earns them praise.

In every park, on every street,
Doggy detectives keep their beat.
For in their world, it's quite a feat,
To sniff out stories that can't be beat.

Whimsical Whiskers and Witty Woofs

In a sunlit park where laughter reigns,
Whiskers wiggle, tickled by gains.
With a wag and a woof, so witty and spry,
They charm the crowds as they leap and fly.

Silly hats on floppy ears,
Bring giggles and glee, not a hint of fears.
Every pounce is a playful jest,
In their furry hearts, they know they're blessed.

Laughter echoes amidst the trees,
As dogs spin 'round with effortless ease.
A chase ensues, then all fall flat,
Rolling in grass, oh, imagine that!

So here's to the pets with souls so bright,
In their amusing world, all feels right.
With whimsical whiskers and joyous woofs,
They spread their cheer from rooftops to roofs.

Pawprints on the Path of Chatter

In the early morn, on a sunbeam path,
Dogs leave pawprints like footprints of math.
With each tiny mark, they share a thought,
Of grand adventures and battles fought.

Soaking in sunlight, their tails wave high,
Every woof a hearty, happy sigh.
With friends beside them, they blabber and play,
The joys of the day chase worries away.

As birds chirp tunes in a funny duet,
Canines strut proudly, no sign of regret.
Their chatter fills the air with a song,
In this joyous world, where they all belong.

Thus, tread softly on this trail of fun,
Where laughter and barks chase away the sun.
Each pawprint tells a story, so nice,
In the book of friendship, it suffices.

Furry Whispers in the Night

In shadows soft, they wiggle and prance,
Tiny paws dancing, a curious dance.
Whispers of mischief tickle the air,
As giggles echo, without a care.

Squirrels taunt from branches high above,
With yips and yaps, they share their love.
A chorus of barks from the canine crew,
In the moonlight glow, the laughter flew.

They scheme for snacks, a secret delight,
Hatching plans in the still of the night.
With wags and jumps, they trip over tails,
Furry companions, their chatter unveils.

Under the stars, their spirits ignite,
In furry whispers, they share their plight.
Who stole the bone? Who dug the hole?
With playful hearts, they're on a stroll.

Howls and Giggles Under the Moon

Under the glow of a silvery light,
They gather around, a furry delight.
With howls that echo, they start their spree,
As laughter erupts from the tallest tree.

Paw prints gather on the soft, cool grass,
While tails wag wildly as friendships amass.
They plot and they plan, in the deep of the night,
Barking with glee, a whimsical sight.

Chasing each other, they spin and they whirl,
With giggles and yips, watch their tails curl.
In this silly play, no worries in sight,
Howls and giggles bring joy to the night.

As the moon winks down on the furry parade,
Their laughter like music, a joyful serenade.
In the warmth of the night, they snuggle up tight,
With dreams that are filled with pure doggy delight.

Canine Chatter on the Wind

With noses to the ground, they gossip and share,
Secrets of squirrels darting midair.
Each wag of the tail tells tales on repeat,
Barking with laughter, oh, what a treat!

Sidewalks transform into runways galore,
As each pup prances, they strut and they score.
Who wore the best bow? Who has the best bark?
Canine chatter lights up the park.

From puddles to pines, their banter runs free,
A chatter that dances, just like a spree.
With silly antics and wise puppy eyes,
Every bark holds a tale, a sweet surprise.

In every whisper, there's joy on the breeze,
Canine chatter, a chorus to please.
Together they romp 'neath the wide-open skies,
With friendship that sparkles, oh how it flies!

Tails that Tell Tales

Those wagging tails have stories to weave,
Whispers of playtimes that they believe.
An epic quest for the squishy toy,
Tails that tell tales of whimsy and joy.

Furry friends gather 'round for a chat,
Exchanging their secrets, just like that.
A squirrel's sly leap, a neighbor's old cat,
Their tales spin around, imagine that!

In laughter and barks, their stories unfold,
Of daring adventures, both brave and bold.
With a tilt of their heads, they ponder the night,
As tails tell tales, everything feels right.

Through sniffs and quick spins, their history flows,
In every wag, their rich humor glows.
So gather your tails, let the tales take flight,
In a world full of barks, we find pure delight!

Tails of Timber Tales

In the forest, a giggle rolls,
As the squirrels all call their goals.
A wily raccoon, with a cheeky flair,
Jumps on a branch, does a three-point chair.

A bear with a wig shakes his head,
While a fox sings loudly, feeling well-fed.
The owls hoot laughs, a night-time choir,
As the moon starts to glow, hearts lift higher.

A deer in a tutu, prancing with glee,
Spins in circles near a tall pine tree.
While rabbits do breakdancing moves in a row,
Nature's own party, the best show to go!

With every twist and every twist,
The trees sway along, they can't resist.
Leaves rustle with mirth, a soft, sweet laugh,
These timber tales craft the best kind of path.

Echoes in the Canopy

Swinging from branches, the monkeys jest,
Telling tall tales, they're simply the best.
A parrot squawks jokes, colorful and loud,
While the old grey owl looks smug but proud.

Down below, a turtle, slow as can be,
Wags his little tail, quite comically.
A lizard wears glasses, reading a book,
While teetering frogs give the ground a good look.

The breeze carries laughter, through leaf and cloud,
As nature's own comedians gather a crowd.
Every echo a giggle, a pun and a tease,
In this canopy stage, it's all meant to please.

So settle back, watch the antics unfold,
Where stories are shared, and laughter isn't sold.
It's a tapestry of joy, a whimsical spree,
In the great green theater, come laugh with me!

Paws Upon the Path

Two puppies in sneakers run with delight,
Chasing each other and yapping at night.
A hedgehog on wheels joins in with a squeak,
While a butterfly dances, playful and sleek.

With every patter, there's mischief afoot,
A raccoon brings snacks, wearing a cute hat.
They tumble and roll, down the gentle hill,
While frogs croak their tunes, adding to the thrill.

A squirrel throws acorns like a jester's tricks,
While birds chirp chorus—nature's silly mix.
The trees are all giggling, swaying in cheer,
As paws make a path, bringing joy far and near.

So skip along, friends, take a moment to laugh,
As twilight draws near on this playful path.
The world is a playground, filled with such glee,
A furry adventure, come join—just be free!

The Great Dogwood Dialogue

In the shade of dogwoods, a debate breaks out,
Who's the best dancer? They argue, no doubt.
A bouncy collie shows off his flair,
While a pit bull jigs with an elegant air.

A tiny Chihuahua joins in the fun,
With moves so absurd, she steals everyone.
They circle around, painting joy in the grass,
Creating a spectacle, each pup brings a class.

An old golden retriever adds to the mix,
With tales of his youth and a few clever tricks.
The dogwood tree chuckles, its branches do sway,
As laughter erupts, turning night into day.

So gather, all canines, don't miss out the cheer,
For the great dogwood dialogue begins here.
It's a paw-some exchange of humor and pride,
In this playful spectacle, let's all take a ride!

An Ode to Our Four-Legged Friends

In the park they prance with glee,
Chasing tails, oh what a spree!
With floppy ears and bouncy steps,
Life's a game, they're the adept.

They dig for treasure, find a shoe,
Claiming spots, quite bold and new.
Slobbery kisses, playful nips,
Fur-covered love in joyful skips.

Watch them wrangle, roll in grass,
Tongues out wide, they race and pass.
With woofs and wags, they tell their tales,
In every heartbeat, joy prevails.

Through muddy puddles they leap and bound,
In their world, pure joy is found.
With every bark, a laugh they bring,
In our hearts, they reign like kings.

Tails Tall and Small

There's a bounce in every tail,
Short or long, they leave a trail.
A poodle prances, struts with pride,
While a bulldog waddles, oh what a ride!

With a yip and a wag so grand,
They chase the squirrels, take a stand.
From tiny yappers to giants bold,
Each one has stories to be told.

In the backyard, a race begins,
Who can catch the frisbee that spins?
With gleaming eyes and floppy ears,
They turn our frowns to giggly cheers.

Every tilt of head, a mystery,
In their little world, such history.
With laughter echoed in their play,
They make our worries float away.

Whispers of the Whispering Woods

In the woods where laughter calls,
Rustling leaves and playful brawls.
A tail flicks low, a paw pounced high,
As woodland creatures scurry by.

A squirrel squirms, a raccoon peeks,
What curious eyes, what funny sneaks!
With every rustle, laughter grows,
The forest hums with joyful shows.

A game of chase beneath the trees,
Echoes of bark carried by the breeze.
With twinkling eyes and leaps of glee,
Nature holds its comedy.

As day gives way to starlit nights,
In covered up spots, they find delights.
Whispering woods, a stage so grand,
For every giggle in furry band.

Laughter in the Leaves

A crunching sound beneath their paws,
As they dart off without a pause.
Through piles of leaves, a joyful splash,
Watch them dive, oh what a dash!

With goofy glances, they stumble and roll,
Every leap, a sight to behold.
In autumn's embrace, they're full of cheer,
Chasing shadows, never fear.

Leaves twirl down like confetti bright,
As four-legged pals take flight.
Their laughter echoes, wild and free,
Nature's jesters with glee at the spree.

So here's to friends with wagging tails,
In a world of mischief, their joy prevails.
With every twist, with every turn,
In their easy joy, we all learn.

Snouts and Secrets Under Stars

Two snouts twitch in the night,
Plotting mischief with delight.
Whispers soft, a playful prank,
Under twinkling stars, they prank.

Paws shuffle, laughter in the air,
Chasing shadows, a bold affair.
Secrets shared in soft moonlight,
With a howl, they give a fright.

Every sniff is a new tale spun,
From squirrel chases to just plain fun.
A pact made under the celestial dome,
Together forever, they're never alone.

Woofs of Wisdom in the Wilderness

In the woods where mischief reigns,
A wise old mutt shares his gains.
"Never chase that silly tail,"
"Trust me now, you'll surely fail."

With a wink and a wag of his ear,
He tells tales to all who can hear.
"Life's like a stick, throw it right,
Catch the joy, then take flight."

Frolicking mutts absorb the lore,
Learning lessons, always wanting more.
With each woof, wisdom's imparts,
In the wild, they steal our hearts.

A Symphony of Sniffs and Barks

A cacophony of cheerful yaps,
Friends unite in playful naps.
Together they dash through the grass,
Composing tunes as the moments pass.

With each sniff, a note they find,
In the song of life, sweet and kind.
They harmonize under the sun,
Every woof tells tales of fun.

A symphony of tails that sway,
In this orchestra, they play away.
As moonlight falls, they serenade,
In a melody of joy, never to fade.

Whiskered Wit in the Park

In the park where the sun shines bright,
Whiskered faces filled with delight.
They trot and tumble, paws a-race,
With laughter in their furry embrace.

A playful pup gives a cheeky grin,
As a wise old hound rolls in the spin.
They share jokes that flutter through air,
With wagging tails and a jaunty flair.

Laughter echoes from one to another,
In the canine world, we are but brothers.
Each chuckle barks a joyful tune,
In this laughter, we bask till noon.

Snouts, Shadows, and Stories

Snouts peek from behind the door,
Curious eyes that long for more.
With every sniff, a tale unfolds,
Of backyard treasures and secrets told.

Shadows dance on the sunlit grass,
Joyful paws in a game they pass.
A wagging tale, a playful leap,
As they whisper secrets, never to keep.

Stories sprout with each bark and sniff,
Of squirrels caught and that dangerous cliff.
They giggle in rhythms, tails all a-swish,
Creating laughter, it's their one true wish.

So gather round, bring a treat or two,
For tales galore are waiting for you.
With snouts and shadows, the fun's alive,
In this wild world where their spirits thrive.

Echoes of the Earthbound

In the morning light, they bounce and romp,
Their bursts of joy make shadows stamp.
Echoes resound in the whispering breeze,
As they chase their dreams with boundless ease.

With a wagging tail and a quizzical gaze,
They dive into mischief like daring rays.
Chasing shadows, they tumble and roll,
In games of laughter, their hearts are whole.

Paw prints sketch stories on paths of mud,
Each tiny adventure a ripple, a thud.
Through giggles and barks, the day unfolds,
In the world of the earthbound, life never grows old.

Ultimately, the echoes grow loud and proud,
A symphony of joy, a jubilant crowd.
With each little bark, they weave their own song,
In the heart of the earthbound where all can belong.

The Paws of Time

Paws that patter through memories bright,
Furry clocks tick, day turns to night.
With every chase and every frolic,
They capture moments, oh so colic!

In the backyard, time skips like a stone,
As they venture into worlds of their own.
A whispering breeze tells tales anew,
Of time gone by, yet still in view.

Oh, how they scamper, and how they prance,
In a world alive with a playful dance.
Each wagging tail tells a story divine,
Marking the moments, oh the paws of time!

As the sun sets low and the stars ignite,
Their laughter lingers in the soft twilight.
For every laugh, a tail will spin,
In the paws of time, joy will always win.

Whirling Tails and Tales

Whirling tails like windswept leaves,
Spin stories of joy, as imagination weaves.
Round and round, in circles they twirl,
Creating a wonderland, a magical swirl.

With every pounce, a tale comes to life,
Of daring adventures and playful strife.
They romp in laughter, in leaps and bounds,
In the heart of the moment, true joy always pounds.

A nudge here, a bark there, the mischief's afoot,
As they teeter and dash in their furry pursuit.
These whirling tails hold secrets untold,
In a whirlwind of fun, watch the stories unfold.

So grab a treat and join in their spree,
For the whirling tales are best shared, you see.
In the spinning chaos of play and delight,
The laughter of friends makes every day bright.

Hidden Whispers of the Wild

In the thicket where shadows play,
Squirrels gossip by the bay,
With twitching tails and muffled squeaks,
They plot mischief for a week.

Foxes prance with stealthy grace,
While owls spin and spin in place,
Every rustle a secret told,
In the wild where laughter's bold.

A raccoon dons a mask with pride,
While deer observe from their safe side,
Each giggle hidden from the sight,
Nature's jesters, pure delight.

Above it all, the sun peeks through,
A funny world, where antics brew,
In whispers soft, they scheme and chatter,
The wild's own board of playful matter.

The Forest's Furry Friends

Fluffy tails and curvy paws,
Rabbits bounce without a pause,
Chasing shadows in the light,
Every chase a funny sight.

Raccoons raid and giggle loud,
Stealing snacks, oh, how they're proud,
While owls chuckle from their perch,
At all this wild, furry research.

Mice in line, they scamper fast,
Who will giggle, who will last?
A snapshot of this playful crew,
Every move holds laughter's hue.

In the glade where creatures meet,
Laughter flows, oh so sweet,
The forest's friends, they sing and dance,
In a world where joy finds a chance.

Tales of the Tail-Wagging Tribe

A wagging tail here, a hopeful glance,
Puppies swirl in a happy dance,
They bark their dreams into the sky,
While chasing butterflies flying high.

Gather 'round, the furry clan,
Each one working on a plan,
To find the best stick in the park,
And have a blast until it's dark.

Batting paws and joyful barks,
Tails a-wag beneath the larks,
They share their treats, their toys, their bliss,
In every woof, a laugh, a kiss.

Under stars, they lie and snore,
With dreams of mischief, they explore,
The tail-wagging tribe, hear their glee,
In the moonlight, wild and free.

Barking at the Breeze

Chasing whispers on the wind,
Their wild parade has begun to spin,
With joyful yaps they sing their tune,
As the sun greets the silver moon.

Clouds above play peek-a-boo,
While canine friends race two by two,
Each pounce on grass, a giggly feat,
With every bark, they shake their feet.

A gust of wind brings scents so sweet,
The furry pack can't handle the heat,
They leap and bound without a care,
With laughter echoing through the air.

In the meadow, they frolic and tease,
Each little yip, a joyous breeze,
For in their hearts, oh can't you see?
Barking at the breeze, wild and free.

Between the Bow and Bough

In the shade where squirrels play,
The branches sway in a silly way.
I hear a giggle from up high,
As leaves flirt with a curious sky.

A dog runs by with a wagging tail,
Chasing dreams, leaving a trail.
He trips on roots, what a sight!
Rolling over, much to delight.

A cat looks down with a knowing grin,
Purring softly, a master of sin.
The high jinks of nature are all around,
Where laughter and barks become unbound.

Under branches, the laughter grows,
With each silly bark that loudly shows.
They dance and prance, oh what a fun,
In the whispers of trees beneath the sun.

Echoed Barks Under the Stars

At midnight hour, the moon takes flight,
With shadows dancing, what a sight!
A chorus rises, woofs and yips,
As sleepy pups shake off their dips.

Each bark topped with a twinkling cheer,
Echoed in laughter for all to hear.
Stars shimmy and sway, lighting the game,
While willow trees join in the fame.

They play tag under the night's cloak,
Creating magic with every poke.
A howling tune, a whispering breeze,
Stitches of joy knit among the trees.

I smile wide at this playful scene,
Where echoes mingle, and all's serene.
In the cradle of twilight, they take the stage,
Unleashing giggles from the sky's page.

Lost in the Labyrinth of Barks

In a maze of whispers, I roam free,
With echoes bouncing, just like a bee.
Every corner hides a furry face,
In this jumbled, joyful, wild space.

Wobbly pups with their floppy ears,
Chasing shadows, banishing fears.
They twirl around, in playful strife,
While tangled tales bring joy to life.

A snort here, a woof there, such delight,
As laughter weaves through the cool night.
In every turn, a surprise awaits,
With wagging tails and curious mates.

I stumble forth, what fun awaits!
In this furry maze, I'll test my fates.
With each bumbled bark, we share the cheer,
Guardians of laughter, never fear!

Fables from Fido's Forest

In Fido's realm where stories weave,
Whiskered legends turn up their sleeves.
A tale of mischief takes its flight,
With paws that dance in the pale moonlight.

The fox tells tales with a clever spin,
Of daring deeds that make heads spin.
A wagging tail becomes the star,
As laughter echoes from near and far.

When owls hoot in their gentle grace,
The dogs perform with a comic face.
Each bark a chapter, filled with glee,
In this fanciful world, wild and free.

So gather 'round as the night unrolls,
With furry fables warming our souls.
In Fido's forest, laughter reigns,
A merry escape from all life's chains.

Nature's Chorus of Canines

In the park, they prance with glee,
Chasing tails beneath the tree.
Some dig holes, while others play,
Barking songs in a joyful array.

The squirrels tease from high above,
With cheeky grins and a dash of love.
Collars jingling, they form a band,
Creating tunes across the land.

With floppy ears and wagging tails,
Their laughter echoes, never fails.
Sliding down the grassy hills,
Their joyous barks give us the thrills.

But hush a moment, what's that there?
A postman approaches, beware, beware!
With every bark, they share the lore,
Of furry legends, we can't ignore.

Whiskers in the Wind

Whiskers twitching, noses in the breeze,
Chasing scents with the greatest of ease.
With fluffy tails raised high above,
They twirl and spin—what a sight of love!

Each gathering bark, a secret code,
Communicating from their little abode.
They leap and roll, in sunlit beams,
Life for them is a world of dreams.

Oh, to be a pup in play,
Where every moment is a holiday.
Full of antics and silly growls,
They bring us laughter, delight, and howls.

With playful barks and some fun races,
In this furry world, joy embraces.
As the sun sets, they rest their heads,
Dreaming of bones and cozy beds.

Pawed Ponderings Beneath the Pines

Pawed footprints in the soft, damp earth,
Wondering what the squirrels are worth.
With curious pokes and gentle snuffs,
They seek adventure, never enough.

Under towering pines, they ponder life,
Imagining worlds free of strife.
They wag and wiggle, in thoughtful repose,
Lost in the wonders that nature bestows.

Their playful minds chase a butterfly,
With leaps and bounds, oh my, oh my!
A dandelion, they want to catch,
But always fall in a comical patch.

Amidst the rustle, a bark so loud,
Declaring, "I'm here!" to nature's crowd.
With every sniff, they write their tales,
Creating laughter that never fails.

Canines in the Canopy

High above, the branches sway,
While canines cheer and frolic away.
They leap with joy from leaf to leaf,
Life's pure magic, bringing relief.

With puppy grins and muddy paws,
They dash through nature, applause, applause!
Every rustle holds a new surprise,
As they pen stories beneath the skies.

Squirrels scamper, with twinkle toes,
As canine friends find new ways to pose.
In the canopy, fun never wanes,
Their playful spirits set the gains!

A symphony of howls fills the air,
In this furry realm, there's love to spare.
With tails a-wagging, they climb the trees,
Life's a giggle, topped off with a breeze.

Fur and Fable

In the park, a pup goes 'woof',
Chasing tales that twist and swoof.
With every leap, a story spins,
Each wag a tale where fun begins.

Squirrels chatter from the trees,
While tails wag like a gentle breeze.
Fetch the stick, oh what a sight,
Who knew such joy could bring delight!

Every furball holds a dream,
Each bark, a laugh, or so it seems.
Rolling in grass, gleeful glee,
A saga told by you and me.

So let's spread joy, not a frown,
In this furry kingdom, we wear the crown!
With paws and laughs, we take our place,
In the wild world of a furry race.

Barking at the Moonlit Sky

Howling at the big, bright moon,
The dogs unite in a funny tune.
One jumps high and takes the lead,
While others join, they're sure to heed.

Crazy echoes fill the air,
Each bark rings out without a care.
A serenade of tails and paws,
Join this choir without a pause!

A raccoon looks, mildly perplexed,
While cats watch on, feeling vexed.
But up they sing, oh what a cheer,
For furry friends, they have no fear!

In the night, they're kings and queens,
Of the park, beneath the evergreen.
So if you hear a raucous sound,
Know that joy and fun abound!

The Language of Leaves

Rustling leaves in a playful breeze,
Pups converse with giggles and tease.
A sniff, a nudge, a wagging tail,
Their whispers tell a curious tale.

In circles, they twirl, as if to dance,
Chasing shadows, they take a chance.
With every tumble, every play,
Leaves flutter down in a joyful sway.

Paw prints left in nature's book,
On branches high, they'll take a look.
Together they prance, a furry crew,
In a world where friendships grow anew.

So let them frolic, let them play,
In the leafy realm, they'll stay all day.
For in this game, we see the truth,
In every bark lies the heart of youth.

A Symphony of Snouts

In a garden of giggles, joy does rise,
With snouts a-wiggling and wide-eyed surprise.
Each woof a note, sharp and bright,
Melody of mischief, pure delight!

A juggler at heart, a pup holds sway,
Tossing toys in a playful display.
With every catch, the crowd goes 'wow',
In this performance, they take a bow.

A symphony woven, from paws to snouts,
As laughter and barks are what it's about.
With silly antics and tricks galore,
The curtain falls, but they ask for more!

So gather round for this snouty show,
Where fun and friendship forever flow.
With every paw's tap, the rhythm stays,
In this merry dance, they'll spend their days.

Canopy Chatter

In the branches, critters jest,
Squirrels tease, they know how to test.
With acorns tossed, a playful fling,
Echoes of laughter in the spring.

Parrots squawk, their jokes are loud,
Swinging high, we cheer the crowd.
Twigs snapping, a dance so quirky,
Nature's comedy, not so murky.

Raccoons peek with a cheeky grin,
Joining in the fun, let's begin!
Chasing shadows, a game of tag,
Who will fall? Oh, what a wag!

Underneath the leafy dome,
Everyone feels right at home.
As sunlight paints a playful scene,
It's a circus fit for a queen!

Pawprints in the Pine

Pawprints lead through the tall trees,
A canine crew with graceful ease.
Chasing tails, what joyful sights,
Around the pines, in afternoon lights.

Furry friends with goofy grins,
Share the stories of their wins.
Rolling green, oh what a treat,
Nature's stage, where joy and play meet.

A squirrel darts, so quick and spry,
Watch the dogs leap, oh, my oh my!
With barks and howls, they join the race,
Pawprints left in a happy place.

At twilight's call, beneath the stars,
Tired tails flop like fallen cars.
In dreams they run, in fields so fine,
Whispers of fun on the forest line!

The Treetop Talkers

Among the leaves, the chatter flows,
Gossip and jokes, as everyone knows.
Little birds poke fun at their mates,
Feathered mischief in their crates.

Monkeys swing with silly flair,
Nuts and berries flying through the air.
Their antics make the branches sway,
As laughter echoes through the day.

A wise old owl, with a knowing glance,
Joins the chorus in a merry dance.
With a hoot and a wink, he takes his part,
In the show of joy, pure from the heart.

Beneath the moon, when stars all gleam,
The treetop talkers share a dream.
A night of stories, wild and bright,
In nature's theater, what a sight!

Rustic Ramblings

On the path where wildflowers bloom,
Critters gather, dispelling gloom.
Chippers chat with a nutty jest,
Finding humor is the best.

Down by the creek, frogs croak in tune,
Making ripples under the moon.
With leaps they share a splashy cheer,
Their antics bring good vibes near.

In the barn, the goats prance and play,
Each one has a joke, come what may.
With playful nibbles and headbutts too,
They turn a dull day into a zoo.

As sunset drapes the fields in gold,
The rustic tales of joy unfold.
In nature's embrace, laughter reigns,
In every corner, happiness gains!

Barking in the Breeze

In the park, the pups all play,
Chasing shadows, come what may.
With wagging tails and playful leaps,
They bark their secrets, no one keeps.

A squirrel darts, a wild dash,
Woofs erupt, a joyful clash.
Tails spin like little propellers,
Each bark's a joke from furry fellas.

Sunshine glints on fur so bright,
Laughter echoes, pure delight.
Paws dance lightly on the grass,
In this game, no time to pass.

As evening falls, they start to rest,
Dreaming dreams of playful quests.
With soft snores beneath the trees,
They're the kings of the summer breeze.

Constellations of Canines

Under the stars, they gather round,
A circle of pups, laughter abound.
With howls that mimic the moon's soft glow,
They share their tales, each pup's a pro.

One claims he chased a comet bright,
Another woofs of a meteor flight.
They pant and giggle, paws in the air,
Spinning tales without a care.

The big Mastiff talks of a starry race,
While a tiny Chihuahua joins the chase.
A bark erupts, a giggle ensues,
Each woof a gem, no one can refuse.

In this cosmic furball, friendships sprout,
Among the stars, there's never doubt.
With every bark, a wish takes flight,
Canine constellations shine so bright.

Woodland Woofs

In a forest deep, where the tall trees sway,
Puppies frolic in a furry ballet.
With every woof, the branches shake,
Nature's rhythm, a barky quake.

Squirrels chatter, a curious crowd,
Pawprints zigzag, they laugh out loud.
One pup stumbles, a tumbling fall,
As laughter rings through the forest hall.

The trees whisper secrets in leafy tones,
As wild canines make silly groans.
A chorus of woofs fills the air,
In this woodland nook, life is rare.

With noses exploring every nook,
They craft their stories like a book.
Tales of adventure, tails in the breeze,
Together they romp with effortless ease.

Tree Trunk Tales

Beside an oak, they lean and plot,
Furry friends, all tangled in thought.
With wiggly tails, they exchange their dreams,
Whispers of biscuits beneath moonbeams.

One pup declares, "I'll climb so high!"
As another scoffs, "You wouldn't even try!"
Barks of laughter, a joyful din,
As they scheme and giggle with grins so wide.

Underneath the bark, tales unfold,
Of great escapes and treats untold.
Each woof a punchline, each tail a tease,
Their friendship blooms like autumn leaves.

With tree trunks as stages, they dance and prance,
In their furry world, there's always a chance.
To tell a tale, or start a game,
Each cozy woof ignites a flame.

Secrets in the Shade

Under leafy boughs, we plot and scheme,
Whispers of mischief, a canine dream.
Squirrels are spies, they chatter away,
While we dig secrets in soft, cool clay.

Shadowy corners hold tales untold,
With tails wagging wildly, we're brave, we're bold.
A stick's not just wood, it's a treasure chest,
We'll guard it with barks—oh, we're truly the best!

The grass is a stage for our playful schtick,
As we leap and we bound, quick as a flick.
Invisible worlds in a small patch of sun,
Life's just more fun when you're fetching for fun!

So gather, my friends, in this shady delight,
With laughter and growls, we'll frolic till night.
Secrets we share beneath branches so wide,
In the heart of the shade, our joy won't subside.

Howls Among the Hollies

Up in the hollies, we gather around,
With yips and with yaps, the laughter is found.
Moonlit mischief is calling our name,
As we join in a chorus, we dance like the flame.

Howls roll like thunder, but it's all in good fun,
We're the friends of the night, the trouble we've spun.
Each branch is a stage, each bush is a seat,
For the hilarious tales of our four-footed fleet.

A rustle, a scamper, what's that in the glade?
A squirrel in disguise? Or a clever charade?
With giggles and growls, we spring into play,
In the kingdom of hollies, we rule come what may!

So howl, my dear pals, till the moon starts to fade,
Our laughter and frolics an unending parade.
In the night's gentle grip, we won't be alone,
For howls among hollies, are hearts set to roam.

Sniffing Out Stories

With noses to ground, we commence our great quest,
Pigments of puddles, we're keen, we're obsessed.
Each whiff's a new tale from the world's bustling sprawl,

We gather the gossip, we're sniffers of all!

A patch on a sidewalk, a scent to explore,
Has someone been here, or is this an old score?
With wags and with wiggles, we search for the clue,
In the land of adventures, there's always more to ensue.

From the park to the porch, our noses are keen,
Tracking down stories—oh, what could it mean?
From picnics to puddles, we uncover delight,
With each little whiff, we bring tales to light.

So let's roam the streets, in a sniffing parade,
Each story unearthed is a memory made.
With pawprints and capers, we'll carve out our lore,
Sniffing out stories is what we adore!

Rumbles in the Roots

Deep in the roots where the earth shakes and rolls,
We find all the treasures that fill our doggy souls.
The rumble of laughter, a giggle, a snort,
As we tumble and tumble, we're never on short.

With muddy paws dancing, we celebrate life,
Jumpy and jolly, away with all strife.
The shadows weave magic, our tails in a twist,
In the roots' hidden secrets, we twirl and we twist.

Bounding through brambles, we leap with delight,
Creating our chaos under moon's gentle light.
In this wild little world, we're the rulers of play,
With rumbles of joy guiding us on our way.

So gather, dear friends, where the roots intertwine,
In the laughter of play, our spirits align.
With barks full of giggles and howls full of cheer,
Rumbles in the roots bring our happiness near.

Laughter Among the Leaves

Under the shade, squirrels conspire,
Chasing their tails, they never tire.
Leaves dance above with a giggling sound,
Nature's comedy, all around.

Sunlight winks through branches wide,
Creating shadows where critters hide.
Each rustle a punchline, each flap a cheer,
In this leafy world, laughter is near.

Twirling around with a playful breeze,
Whispers of humor hang from the trees.
The world seems bright when you wear a grin,
With laughter echoing from within.

So come join the fun in this merry glade,
Where every creature has a joke to trade.
Life is a stage, and joy sets the scene,
In this forest of fun, we reign supreme.

Whiskers in the Wilderness

Whiskers twitch as they plot their schemes,
Adventurous felines live out wild dreams.
Pouncing through brambles, they joyfully leap,
While nesting birds chirp their secrets to keep.

A butterfly lands, and the chase is on,
Through tall grass they dash, from dusk till dawn.
With each tiny pounce, they sniff out delight,
In the wilderness where mischief ignites.

Hiding in shadows, they plot and they play,
A game of tag in the bright light of day.
With tails held high and eyes full of glee,
These whiskered adventurers are wild and free.

When the sun sets low, their cavorting does cease,
They curl up snug in the warmth of the peace.
Dreaming of capers under starry skies,
Tomorrow begins with new, playful lies.

Rustle of the Realms

In every corner, a rustle, a chirp,
Creatures giggle, oh how they burp!
From bushes and thickets, the grins unfold,
A symphony of laughter, both brave and bold.

Tiny feet scurry, on a merry chase,
Through gardens and meadows, they dash with grace.
Nature's own stage, where antics abound,
With a thump and a bounce, laughter resounds.

Frogs leap up, with silly croaks,
Each little hop, a joke that evokes.
In the twilight glow, their antics are clear,
The woodland's joy is a gift we hold dear.

So gather the chuckles and let them take flight,
With rustling whispers that spark pure delight.
In realms of the wild, where fun's always found,
The heart of the forest is laughter unbound.

Paws, Ponderings, and Poems

Paws patter softly on the garden floor,
Curious critters in search of more.
Chasing their tails in the afternoon sun,
Each giggle they share, a treasure spun.

With a pounce and a wiggle, the mischief begins,
A paw reaches out, and the laughter spins.
In a world of whimsy, where fun is the rule,
Every glance exchanged is a playful duel.

Under the boughs where secret tales thrive,
Nature's playground keeps silliness alive.
Two furry friends trade their thoughts with delight,
In this paws and ponderings, joy feels just right.

So write us a poem, let silliness flow,
Each line a reminder that giggles can grow.
In the company of friends, our hearts take to flight,
As paws, ponderings, and dreams dance through night.

Poems

Crafting a verse, how playful can we get?
With each line a chuckle, no cause for regret.
Scribbling stories of joyful escapes,
In a world that's bright with laughter in shapes.

Nature's own jesters, with antics to share,
Each stanza a witness to merriment rare.
Frogs, squirrels, and owls, all join in the fun,
As we spin our yarns beneath the warm sun.

Playful and silly, let creativity fly,
In every small moment, let giggles comply.
For in the great tapestry of life's silly seams,
We find our own laughter woven in dreams.

Crescendo of Canine Conversations

In the park they chatter, tails in a twirl,
"Did you see that squirrel?" in a happy whirl.
Paws stomp the ground, as they share a tale,
With woofs and barks, they never seem pale.

A yap about dinners served in bowls,
"I prefer the treats, they fill my soul!"
Noses twitching, the gossip spreads wide,
In their raucous reunion, they take such pride.

Oh, the tales of the mailman, quite the jest,
He runs like the wind, they're all quite impressed.
Each doggy delight, a bark filled with cheer,
In this furry symposium, laughter's sincere.

As sunset nears, their chatter subsides,
With a final woof, each pup barks with pride.
Tomorrow brings new tales to ignite,
In a world of fur, laughter takes flight.

Laughs in Leashes

Tangled in leashes, they race side by side,
With a sniff and a snort, it's a comical ride.
"Who gets the treat?" is the debate of the day,
As their humans just chuckle, watching the play.

One pup takes a leap, as if on a quest,
"I'm king of the park!" he barks with zest.
The others roll over, in fits of delight,
Creating a spectacle—a hilarious sight.

With tongues out and tails all a-wag,
They swap silly stories, it's never a drag.
"Remember the time I caught that big branch?"
"Not even close! You should've seen my dance!"

As daylight fades, the laughter is bright,
In this canine circus, they own the night.
Every bark is a giggle, in a playful embrace,
Friendships in wagging, a joyful race.

Friendships Forged in Fur

Two pups play fetch, both eager to win,
"I'll bring it back first!" with a playful grin.
The audience of birds can only just stare,
At this furry showdown, a light-hearted fare.

When playtime concludes, it's time for a chat,
They gossip and giggle, as only friends can at.
"What a catch today! I'm really the best,
By the way, did I mention I never take rest?"

They share bones and tales of who went astray,
While chasing each other, in a loose ballet.
With wags as their anchors, their laughter is loud,
In this canine club, they're eternally proud.

As the sun dips low, and shadows grow long,
Their spirits remain high, with love as their song.
In the laughter of fur, bonds are designed,
Forever together, endlessly aligned.

Echoes of Playful Prowess

Amidst bouncing pups, there's a raucous cheer,
Each bark like a note, music to their ear.
They race through the grass, with glee in their stride,
With pounces and tumbles, their joy they can't hide.

"Do you see that ball? I can catch it with flair!"
"I can leap higher, just look at my air!"
With playful debates, they heighten the fun,
In this contest of joy, there's no need to run.

When nap time calls, it's a snuggle parade,
Brought closer together, their antics won't fade.
"Tell me a story about yesterday's chase,"
With furry giggles echoing, they find their place.

As twilight descends, and adventure does wane,
They share all their treasures, a light-hearted gain.
In their world of frolic, where fun knows no end,
The laughter continues—these pups, they're a blend.

The Grove's Gentle Murmur

In the grove where shadows play,
Whiskered friends have much to say.
They gossip loud, they joke and tease,
Nature's laughter sways the trees.

With tails a-wagging, puffs of air,
Chasing squirrels without a care.
A playful nudge, a cheeky grin,
Join the fun, let games begin!

Under boughs, their stories flow,
Chasing after dreams aglow.
Every bark a tune to sing,
In this land of joy, they spring.

Among the leaves, their laughter swells,
In goofy faces, joy compels.
With tongue outstretched and eyes so bright,
They turn each moment into light.

Canine Communique

Woofer whispers, paws that dance,
With wagging tails, they forge romance.
A yip for joy, a howl for fun,
Each little bark like sunshine won.

On the lawn where friendships bloom,
Puppy pranks dispel the gloom.
With a roll and playful hop,
They spin like tops, just never stop!

Scented secrets in the air,
Trading tales with charming flair.
A playful nip, a gentle growl,
In their world, there's always howl.

Through muddy paths and meadows green,
Every canine king and queen.
With paws that patter on the ground,
In laughter's echo, joy is found.

The Chronicles of the Canines

Gather 'round for tails of gold,
Where pup adventures all unfold.
From chasing tails to barking loud,
Each canine tale makes us proud.

In the park where squirrels tease,
Oh, how they tumble, roll, and freeze!
With noses wet, and eyes aglow,
Every quest leads where they go.

With each woof, the stories grow,
Chasing dreams, they steal the show.
Through every zig and every zag,
They strut with pride, they're such a rag!

In cozy nooks and sunny rays,
Their antics fill our joyful days.
With a prance, they own the ground,
In their grace, pure love is found.

In the Shade of Companion Clouds

Under canopies of green delight,
Silly friends in purest sight.
With every wiggle, joy abounds,
In carefree moments, laughter sounds.

Nutty games beneath the sun,
Chasing shadows just for fun.
With a woof and playful leap,
In their hearts, no worries creep.

Sliding down on grassy hills,
Each and every joy instills.
With floppy ears and snouts so wide,
They embrace the day with pride.

When clouds drift by, they wag their tails,
In the magic where friendship prevails.
Through every giggle, bark, and cheer,
These joyful souls always near.

Canines and the Color of Leaves

In the park where dogs do play,
Leaves dance in a bright ballet.
A golden retriever leaps so high,
   Chasing shadows in the sky.

Poodles prance in coats of red,
While a beagle sniffs and threads.
Each swirl of color, a playful tease,
The laughter rustles through the trees.

Squirrels scamper, cheeks all stuffed,
Dogs bark back, all huffed and puffed.
With every tail that gleefully wags,
   Nature's laughter never drags.

A tennis ball on pilfered ground,
Leaves get trampled, laughter found.
Canines leap, with joy they weave,
   An autumn tale that won't deceive.

Nature's Nocturnal Narratives

When the moon takes its silver seat,
Dogs gather round with nimble feet.
They howl stories of the night,
In shadows stretching, pure delight.

The owls hoot, the crickets play,
As pups embark on games of stray.
With twinkling eyes and fur so bright,
Each bark echoes in the night.

A shadow pounces, a playful chase,
Tail to tail in a frisky race.
Furry whispers twist the air,
Nocturnal mischief everywhere!

Amidst the stars, their voices rise,
With howls and sniffs beneath the skies.
By dawn, tales of adventure blend,
With doggy dreams that never end.

The Rhythm of Ruffs

In the garden where mischief brews,
Canines gather, each brings views.
A rhythmic bark, a playful sound,
A melody of fun unbound.

From tiny yips to hearty roars,
Each dog's tune opens up doors.
Cavalier king meets the scruffy mutt,
With a wagging tail, their troubles cut.

Paws tap dance on bubbling leaves,
As laughter sings, the spirit weaves.
A chorus of snores echoes at noon,
With playful ruffs, the garden's tune!

In every bark, a joke is found,
As canines chase on shaky ground.
With rumping glee and laughter bright,
Their rhythms make the world feel right.

A Forest Full of Fur

In the forest, fur flies free,
Canines frolic, wild with glee.
Branches sway in joyous bursts,
While puppies quench their playful thirsts.

A collie spins in a leafy swirl,
While a tiny pup begins to twirl.
Muddy paws on bright green grass,
Each joyful bark the trees surpass.

Over logs and through the streams,
Silly antics fuel their dreams.
Underneath the towering pines,
Every pawprint joy defines.

With laughter echoing through the bark,
Canines rule till night is dark.
A forest full of wagging tails,
Where every moment love prevails.

Whispering Woods and Wagging Tails

In the woods where shadows play,
Squirrels chatter, dogs at bay.
Furry friends chase leaves that swirl,
Their tails a wagging, happy whirl.

Barks of laughter crack the trees,
With every leap, they chase the breeze.
Paws that dance on crunchy ground,
Together, joy is always found.

Tiny paws with hearts so bold,
Tales of mischief to be told.
Underneath the starry sky,
Playful woofs and barks will fly.

When the sun sets, games are spun,
In the glade, the night's pure fun.
Each woof a tale, each bark a song,
In this forest where we belong.

The Poetry of Paws

Whiskers twitch as stories weave,
Furry poets, none deceive.
With every leap, a verse they share,
In the rhythm of the air.

Lost in thoughts, they sit and muse,
A scruffy pup with worn-out shoes.
Each tail a stanza, sad or bright,
In the dog park, they ignite the night.

Chasing shadows, barking loud,
They gather 'round in a cheerful crowd.
Paws on grass, they write their prose,
In every sniff, a poem grows.

Together, in this playful jest,
With muddy paws, they love the quest.
For every bark, there's laughter here,
In their hearts, they have no fear.

A Celebration of Canine Characters

Once a pup with spots galore,
Wore a hat, but wanted more.
Imagine paws that dance and twirl,
In their world, they're kings and girls.

There's Benny with a goofy grin,
Who can charm you with a spin.
Fluffing up with every cheer,
His antics make the world so clear.

Martha ponders, wise and sweet,
Every bark, a tasty treat.
With her smarts, she steals the show,
In her heart, friendships grow.

In this crew of funny mates,
Life's a party, never waits.
Let's raise a paw, a toast to all,
Our canine friends, we stand enthralled.

The Adventures of the Woodland Woofers

In the woods, with tails in flight,
Woofers gather, heart's delight.
Leaping over logs and streams,
In their eyes, adventure gleams.

Through the thickets, they explore,
Chasing dreams they can't ignore.
Rustling leaves and playful chases,
Finding joy in secret places.

Silly squirrels with cheeky dart,
Turn the chase into fine art.
Woofers giggle, paws on the go,
Sharing secrets only they know.

Under the sun, they run and play,
Every moment, a bright display.
In their laughter, hearts unite,
Woodland woofers, pure delight.

www.ingramcontent.com/pod-product-compliance
Lightning Source LLC
Chambersburg PA
CBHW051648160426
43209CB00004B/832